THE EDMUND FITZGERALD
Lost With All Hands

A True Story for Young Readers

by

Captain Robert Hertel

River Road Publications, Inc.

Spring Lake, Michigan

Published by River Road Publications, Inc.
830 East Savidge Street, Spring Lake, Michigan 49456-1961.
Printed in the United States of America

Library of Congress Cataloging-in-Publication Data

Hertel, Robert

The Edmund Fitzgerald: lost with all hands; a true story for
young readers/by Captain Robert Hertel

p. cm.

Includes index.

ISBN 0-938682-49-0

1. Edmund Fitzgerald (Ship)—Juvenile literature. 2.
Shipwrecks—Superior, Lake—Juvenile literature. [1. Edmund
Fitzgerald (Ship) 2. Shipwrecks.] I. Title.

G530.E26H47 1998   917.7'49—dc21

98-28320 CIP AC

Table of Contents

Credits

Cover illustration by Don Ellens, Grand Rapids, Michigan

Other photos and illustrations are reproduced through the courtesy of: p. vi, Mary C. Demroske, Mushroom Cap Studio and Gallery, Brimley, Michigan; p. 9, Buffalo and Erie County Historical Society; p. 12, Stephen A. Bastek, United States Coast Guard; p. 16, Great Lakes Marine Collection of the Milwaukee Public Library/Wisconsin Marine Historical Society; p. 24, Lake Michigan Maritime Museum; pp. 35, 36, 41, United States Coast Guard; p. 46, Gail A. Vander Stoep; all other photos and illustrations are the property of River Road Publications, Inc.

The Edmund Fitzgerald

Lost With All Hands

"Superior Duel," a painting by Mary C. Demroske, shows the
Fitzgerald's last night on Lake Superior.

Chapter One

November 10, 1975

It is seven o'clock on the night of November 10, 1975. The *Edmund Fitzgerald*, a 729-foot ship, is in trouble. She is leaking and **listing**; slowly tipping to the side. The wind across Lake Superior is blowing at 60 miles per hour and gusting to over 100 miles per hour. The waves are 25 to 30 feet high. The *Fitzgerald* is nearing a sheltered point and safety when the ship about eight miles behind her, the *Arthur Anderson*, radios the captain of the *Edmund Fitzgerald*, Captain Ernest "Mac" McSorley, to find out how they are doing. Captain McSorley says, "We are holding our own."

Neither man knows that those will be the last words ever heard from the *Edmund Fitzgerald*. The men on the *Arthur Anderson* watch on radar as the *Edmund Fitzgerald* heads into a cloud of snow. Fifteen minutes later the snow clears up, but the *Fitzgerald* is gone.

The Great Lakes form a vast natural waterway. With the help of some canals and locks, it is possible for ships from the Atlantic Ocean to travel inland as far as northeastern Minnesota.

Chapter Two

The Inland Seas

Five connecting lakes make up the Great Lakes of North America. They are Lake Ontario, Lake Erie, Lake Huron, Lake Michigan, and Lake Superior. Together, they are the largest body of fresh water in the world. They are so big, some people call them the Inland Seas.

Lake Superior is the largest, deepest, and farthest north of the five lakes. It is 1,333 feet deep in its deepest spot. At its widest point the lake is 350 miles across from shore to shore. Some sailors prefer Lake Superior over the other lakes because it has more "sea room"; there is less chance of ships being blown ashore. But Lake Superior also allows room for waves to build up and become bigger than they would on other lakes.

The surface of Lake Superior is 600 feet above sea level, or 600 feet higher than the level of the Earth's seas. It is the highest elevation of the Great Lakes. Lake Superior's waters run down through the Saint Mary's River into Lake Huron and Lake Michigan. The waters drop 21 feet as they travel down the Saint Mary's River.

Rapids on the fast moving river make it impossible for boats to navigate it. Before 1855 all **cargo** coming from or going to Lake Superior had to be unloaded, carried around the rapids in the river, and reloaded onto another ship on the other side of the rapids. In 1855 the Soo Locks were built to allow ships to bypass the rapids and travel back and forth between Lake Huron and Lake Superior.

A Great Lakes freighter passes through the Soo Locks.

Lake Huron drains into Lake Erie through Lake St. Clair and the Detroit River. The water drops nine feet between Lake Huron and Lake Erie. No **locks** are needed, however, because the drop is spread over a large area.

The waters of the Great Lakes flow to lower elevations, eventually draining into the Atlantic Ocean.

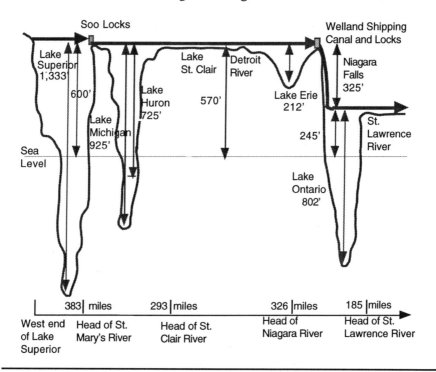

On the east side of Lake Erie, the water drops 325 feet to Lake Ontario. This spectacular drop is Niagara Falls. The **Welland Canal** allows ships in Lake Ontario to travel around the falls to Lake Erie and the other Great Lakes. From Lake Ontario the water runs through seven more locks and over 1,000 miles to the Atlantic Ocean through the St. Lawrence River. Although the first European ships entered this river in the early 1500s, they did not discover the natural Great Lakes waterway for over a century.

Chapter Three

Shipping and Shipwrecks

During the Ice Age the Great Lakes **basin** was covered with glaciers. Over thousands of years the glaciers slowly melted and shrank. The melting glaciers formed the five Great Lakes and created a system of creeks, streams, and rivers to constantly feed the lakes with fresh water. The ice retreated about 4,000 years ago. Life returned to the rich land. Thick forests grew up; fish, birds, and animals came to the Great Lakes and their shores.

Native Americans were the first people to find the Great Lakes. They used canoes to travel the waterways. It was easier to glide on the water than to walk in the thick woods with heavy packs on their backs. They made their canoes of hollowed-out logs. These canoes were called dugout canoes. Some Indians made fast, lightweight canoes from birchbark. They wrapped bark from birch trees around wooden frames and sealed the seams with pitch from pine trees.

Each season entire villages would load into large canoes and travel hundreds of miles to camps where the people fished, hunted, and farmed, depending on the season. For thousands of years the only boats on the Great Lakes were the canoes of the Native Americans.

In the 1600s, Frenchmen began to explore the Great Lakes. They came across the Atlantic Ocean in sailing ships and up the St. Lawrence River as far as the present-day Quebec or Montreal. There the French explorers left their ships behind and continued on with Indian canoes and guides. Most traveled across the region we now call Ontario to Lake Huron.

The French wanted furs from animals to send back to Europe. They traveled all over the Great Lakes and up rivers and streams to trap beaver, muskrat, fox, mink, and other animals with valuable furs. They also traded with the Indians. These Frenchmen were called **voyageurs**. For a long time the voyageurs carried all the furs and other trade goods in canoes.

In the 1670s a French explorer named LaSalle learned from a fur trader that Lake Erie was connected to Lake Huron and Lake Michigan. LaSalle decided to build a sailing ship to travel these lakes. With a large ship he could pick up the furs and drop off supplies to traders all around the three lakes. It would save paddling all those miles in canoes.

LaSalle and his men built a ship at the eastern end of Lake Erie near Niagara Falls and named it the *Griffon*. She was the first ship to sail on the Great Lakes. For her first voyage, LaSalle sailed the *Griffon* from Niagara to

The Griffon was the first sailing ship on the Great Lakes.

Washington Island in northwest Lake Michigan. At
Washington Island his men loaded the ship with furs
and began the return to Niagara. LaSalle stayed behind
to explore the shores of Lake Michigan and the Missis-
sippi River. A great storm blew the next day. The *Griffon*
and her crew were never seen again. The first ship on the
Great Lakes had also become the first shipwreck.

Some people say there have been nearly 10,000
shipwrecks on the Great Lakes. Most of the wrecks were
in the days when ships had only sails. Sailing ships
could not motor away from the shore or rocky reefs. If
the wind blew them toward danger, there was very little
they could do. **"Breakers** ahead!" shouted from **aloft**
often signaled the end of a ship and sometimes her crew.
It meant the ship was headed for shallow water and soon
would run **aground** and break apart.

In the days of sail, **mariners** were on their own on
the Lakes. Skippers had to forecast the weather themselves, using their eyes to judge the clouds moving
through and a wetted finger to observe the wind
direction. While underway, a compass was often the only
navigational instrument they had. **Charts**, if they had
them, were crudely drawn and inaccurate. **Soundings** to

find the depth of water, were taken with a **leadline**, a piece of lead tied to a rope and dropped over the side.

Early sailors had no help along their voyages. There were no lighthouses or other navigational guides to alert them to dangerous **shoals** and peninsulas. In the fog, in snowstorms, or in rough weather with water spraying over the deck, they sailed blind. Some skippers used their

noses to smell the approaching shore. If the ship was in trouble, there was no way to call for help; they had no radios. Neither was there anyone to rescue them.

In the 1800s a few steps were taken to help sailors on the Great Lakes. The

Lighthouses began to be built on the western Great Lakes in the mid-1800s. This one at Sturgeon Point on Lake Huron was built in 1869.

first Great Lakes lighthouse was built on Lake Erie in 1818. However, it was not until 1847 that a lighthouse was built on Lake Superior. In 1871 the first lifesaving crews were formed. These men were trained and paid to launch lifeboats and rescue crew members from a shipwreck.

Captains today have accurate charts and maps which show the shoreline and where the shallow spots are. They also have **radar**. Radar sends out a signal that bounces back to the ship. It shows the shoreline and other ships on a screen much like a television. Radar helps the captain avoid collisions. **Depth sounders** tell the captain how deep the water is under his ship. **Loran C** and the newer **GPS** (Global Positioning System) are electronic devices that let the Captain know the exact position of his ship.

Radios let the captain talk to captains of other ships and to stations on shore which provide information on weather, position, and other important advice for safe passage. If the ship is in trouble, the Captain can use the radio to get help. The Coast Guard has boats, helicopters, and people trained to save the crew if the ship is sinking. All these things make shipping much safer on the Great Lakes now than it was in the past. Still, ships

Today, a U. S. Coast Guard ship, like the 180-foot Sundew, could respond to a ship's distress signal.

can still sink and captains need to respect Great Lakes storms.

In 1958 the *Carl D. Bradley* was making her last run home on Lake Michigan, heading from Gary, Indiana, to Alpena, Michigan. She was rusting badly and was scheduled for repair work that winter. The crew was eager for the shipping season to end and to get home for Christmas. Sadly, only two men made it home. Fighting huge waves in a November storm, the *Bradley* tore in half and went to the bottom. Some of her crew went with her. Others froze to death or drowned in the icy water.

In November, 1966, the *Daniel J. Morrell* was pushing her way through a storm on Lake Huron. She was over sixty-years-old and was made of an old type of steel that is no longer used because it becomes brittle in cold water. The water was very cold. The *Morrell* cracked in half. The back half, containing the engine, steamed off into the dark, lights still blazing. In the cold water only a few men made it onto the life raft. One by one the men died from the cold. Only one man was picked up alive.

November is a month especially feared by Great Lakes sailors. It is the time of year when cold arctic air moves south and mixes with the warm air of autumn. The two air masses begin to spin and create fast winds that whip the water into ferocious waves. Ship owners want the profits from "just one more" run, and so the captains and crews gamble their lives and their ships on completing as many trips as they can before the water freezes and ends another season. The gamble is sometimes lost.

In November 1913, a tremendous storm blew through the Great Lakes. When it was over ten ships had sunk, over twenty ships were thrown ashore, and 235 mariners had lost their lives. One ship, the *Charles S. Price*, was found floating upside down in Lake Huron. Several ships were stranded in the White Fish Bay area during that storm, and one was lost near Marquette.

In November 1940, another deadly storm sank five ships and killed 58 men. Three large freighters went down in Lake Michigan off the coast of Pentwater, Michigan, The *Bradley* and *Morrell* also went down in November storms.

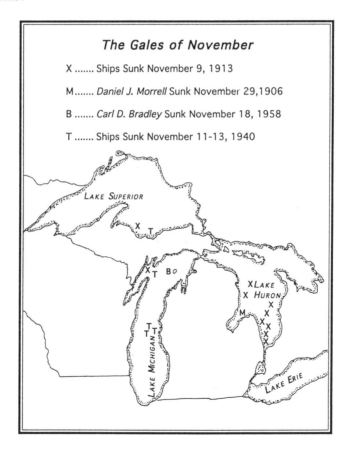

The Gales of November

X .... Ships Sunk November 9, 1913

M .... *Daniel J. Morrell* Sunk November 29, 1906

B .... *Carl D. Bradley* Sunk November 18, 1958

T .... Ships Sunk November 11-13, 1940

The Edmund Fitzgerald is launched in 1958.

Chapter Four

Pride of the Lakes

On June 7, 1958, nearly 10,000 people gathered along the Rouge River just south of Detroit to watch the launch of the longest ship ever built on the Great Lakes. Mrs. Edmund Fitzgerald broke a bottle of champagne over the **bow**, and the huge ship slid down the **ways** and splashed into the river. The ship was named after Mrs. Fitzgerald's husband, Chairman of the Northwestern Mutual Life Insurance Company of Milwaukee. This company owned the *Fitzgerald*. The new ship was 75 feet wide and 729 feet long — longer than two football fields placed end to end. It would fit through the big locks at Sault Ste. Marie with only a few feet to spare.

The *Edmund Fitzgerald* was designed to haul bulk cargo; iron ore, coal, and wheat. During her seventeen years of service she would mainly haul **taconite**, a refined form of iron ore in pellet form. She carried taconite from western Lake Superior to the mills in Detroit and Cleveland on Lake Erie or to Gary, Indiana, at the southern tip of Lake Michigan.

Great Lakes cargo ships usually fill their **ballast** tanks with water in the south. They need the weight to make them stable. They then travel up to seven hundred miles north and west without any cargo. When they reach port in western Lake Superior, the water is pumped out of the ballast tanks and the cargo is poured into the **hold**. Heavily loaded, the ships head **down-bound** to unload. The ships repeat this trip over and over during

Ships like the Fitzgerald still haul taconite from the shores of Lake Superior to cities along the other Great Lakes. Here taconite is being loaded at Marquette, Michigan, on Lake Superior.

the nine or ten month shipping season, creating an efficient and economical way to transport bulk freight from Minnesota and Canada to industrial cities along the southern shores of the Great Lakes.

Over the years Great Lakes vessels have developed a distinct style. They have long flat decks covered with large hatches that are lifted off to load and unload their cargoes. Some ships even have their own crane conveyors for loading and unloading.

At each end of the ship are cabins. In the forward cabin is the pilot house and navigation room. The captain's quarters and rooms for the other officers and crew that steer and operate the ship are also in the forward cabin. Two long tunnels under the main deck lead back to the **aft** or **stern** cabin. The aft cabin has rooms for the engineer and crew who maintain the ship's steam engine, located below them. The kitchen and galley, or dining room, is also located in the stern cabin.

There are many jobs on board ship. Nearly thirty people live and work aboard the ship for the entire season, seldom having over one day in any port. The **captain**, or master, is in charge of the ship. The **first**

Great Lakes cargo ships have a distinctive style. A long cargo area or hold is covered with a flat deck. The foreward and aft cabins contain the crew's quarters and work areas. The drawings illustrate the layout of a typical laker or cargo ship.

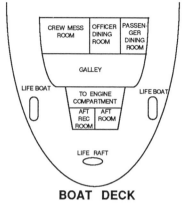

AFT DECKS

BOAT DECK

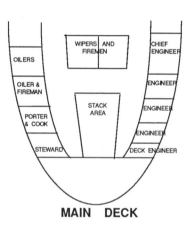

MAIN DECK

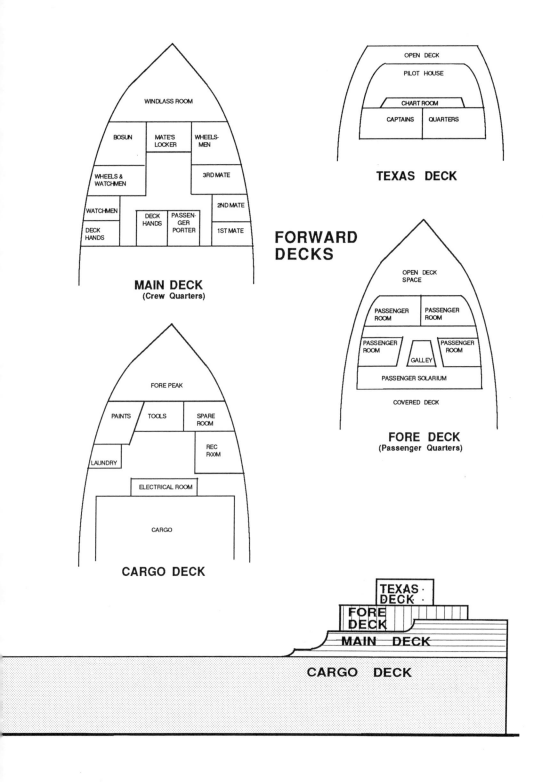

WINDLASS ROOM

BOSUN | MATE'S LOCKER | WHEELS-MEN

WHEELS & WATCHMEN | 3RD MATE

WATCHMEN | DECK HANDS | PASSEN-GER PORTER | 2ND MATE

DECK HANDS | | | 1ST MATE

MAIN DECK
(Crew Quarters)

OPEN DECK

PILOT HOUSE

CHART ROOM

CAPTAINS | QUARTERS

TEXAS DECK

FORWARD DECKS

FORE PEAK

PAINTS | TOOLS | SPARE ROOM

LAUNDRY | | REC ROOM

ELECTRICAL ROOM

CARGO

CARGO DECK

OPEN DECK SPACE

PASSENGER ROOM | PASSENGER ROOM

PASSENGER ROOM | | PASSENGER ROOM

GALLEY

PASSENGER SOLARIUM

COVERED DECK

FORE DECK
(Passenger Quarters)

TEXAS DECK

FORE DECK

MAIN DECK

CARGO DECK

mate is actually second in command and carries out the captain's orders. Second mates and third mates assist the first mate. They make sure the **wheelsmen**, who steer the ship, and the **watch**, who keep a lookout for other ships and boats, do their jobs. An able-bodied maintenance person, also known as a **bosun**, is in charge of the **deckhands**. Deckhands are responsible for the exterior of the ship. They remove and replace the hatches as well as scrape, paint, and repair the outside of the ship.

In the stern of the ship, the **chief engineer** is in charge of the ship's engines. First, second, and third mates to help maintain the engines and boilers. **Wipers** keep the engineroom clean. **Oilers** do the repairs. The first cook and second cook live in cabins close to the kitchen and galley. **Porters** bring the captain and any guests their food. They also clean the quarters of the captain and the guestrooms.

As the *Edmund Fitzgerald* floated in the river, people marveled at her size. She was not only the largest ship now afloat on the Great Lakes, she was also one of the most comfortable. Gone were the days when the crew must all sleep together in the **foc'sle**, a crowded damp cabin in the bow. Now, many of the crew had their own rooms, some with private bathrooms. They were free to decorate as they pleased. Many brought aboard stereos, televisions, pictures for the walls, rugs, anything to make life more comfortable.

For the next seventeen years, the *Edmund Fitzgerald* would be the proudest ship on the Lakes. She quickly began breaking records for the largest cargoes hauled (over 27,000 tons) and the greatest tonnage and most trips for the season. With a 7,000 horsepower engine and a top speed of sixteen **knots** loaded, she was the fastest ore freighter on the lakes. Even when larger and faster ships were later built, sailors still had special feelings for the "Big Fitz" and duty on board her was highly prized. Only the best would be offered a **berth** on her, and those who came aboard would work hard to stay.

The *Fitzgerald's* career was not without some mishaps. She hit the wall of the Soo Locks a couple of times. Once she rammed another ship. She also ran aground in a harbor. But these were fairly routine injuries in the life of a freighter.

The Edmund Fitzgerald - 1957-1975

Chapter Five

The Final Trip

It is November 9, 1975. It is a peaceful, warm Sunday afternoon as the *Edmund Fitzgerald* leaves Superior, Wisconsin. She steams past the breakwater and into Lake Superior with a hold full of taconite. Her regular first cook is disappointed. He has been off the ship with stomach problems, an ulcer, for two weeks. He had hoped to join the ship again before she left port, but this morning his stomach hurt again and his doctor has told him to stay home. He doesn't know it, but the decision saves his life.

About two hours later when the ship is twenty-five miles out of port the National Weather Service announces a **gale** warning for the lake. A gale warning means there could be winds of around forty miles per hour. Captain McSorley, in the pilot house, is not worried; he has sailed for forty-four years. He has a good ship that has been through many gales and heavy seas. His ship was inspected by the Coast Guard only a week ago, and although they found some problems that would need to be fixed during the winter lay-up, she is fit for duty.

A young **cadet** is aboard the *Fitzgerald*. He is probably more nervous than the captain because this is his first season on the Lakes. He is a student, studying to become a ship's mate and is spending time aboard the freighter to gain experience.

At about the same time as the *Fitzgerald* receives the warning, the *Arthur M. Anderson* enters the lake from Two Harbors, Minnesota. She is 767-feet long and also carries a load of taconite. The ships are only about ten miles apart, and the captain of the *Anderson,* Jesse "Bernie" Cooper, calls the *Fitzgerald* on the radio to discuss the approaching bad weather.

The two captains agree to stick together while crossing Lake Superior. They decide that instead of heading straight across, they will take the northern route. The wind is coming from the northeast, and by following the Canadian shore, they hope to avoid the large waves that will build into even bigger waves as the wind whips across the lake. The farther north they stay, the more protected the ships will be from the waves.

Two ships pass each other at the mouth of White Fish Bay.

By midnight, the two ships are twenty-five miles south of Isle Royale. The weather is much worse. The wind is blowing steadily at sixty miles an hour and the average wave is ten feet high. Some are much larger. The gale warning issued earlier is changed to a storm warning.

The *Fitzgerald* and the *Arthur M. Anderson* push on, heading straight into the wind, facing the waves. It is raining hard and is difficult to see. Spray from the waves crashing into the bows of the ships runs down the decks. Still, they continue.

By ten o' clock on the morning of November 10, the wind has died down to forty miles an hour and the waves are smaller. The captains decide that they can now turn east. By noon, the wind is only fifteen miles an hour and the two ships, with the *Fitzgerald* in the lead, turn south.

Both captains know the bad weather is not over. They are now in the eye of the storm. Storms swirl in a counter-clockwise direction, like water drains from a bathtub. In the center it is calm, but all around the center the air is moving very fast. Captain Cooper works up a forecast that shows the other side of the storm will bring winds of almost ninety miles an hour. He thinks he must have made a mistake.

Unfortunately, he hasn't made a mistake. Satellite photos of the powerful storm later showed that it extended as far east as New York and as far south as Florida.

By three o' clock the wind has increased and the waves are up to fifteen feet. It is snowing hard. The *Fitzgerald* is south of Michipoten Island and ready to turn southeast, but there is a problem. Her long-range radar is not working and is turned off. She still has close-range radar, but this does not give a complete and clear picture of the ship's location. The large waves show up on the short-range screen, giving false "targets".

Captain McSorley must know exactly where he is for the next turn. He wants to stay as close as he can to Caribou Island to get protection from the waves, but he must not pass over the Six Fathom Shoals. The water over the **shoals** is only thirty-six feet deep, and the *Fitzgerald* fully loaded draws twenty-seven feet. With the ship rising and falling in the heavy waves, she could hit bottom.

Two charts are used in this area. Oddly, the Canadian and the U.S. charts show the shoals in

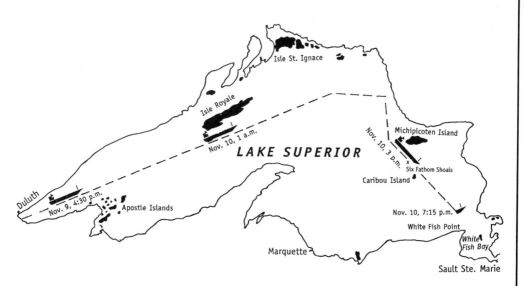

The map shows the final route of the Edmund Fitzgerald.

different places. Later checks showed that neither chart was correct. Captain McSorley, with inaccurate charts and no long-range radar, orders the ship turned.

In the pilot house of the *Anderson*, Captain Cooper and First Mate Morgan Clark watch the *Fitzgerald* on radar. "He sure looks like he's in the shoal area," Clark says. "He's in too close," Captain Cooper agrees. "He's closer than I'd want this ship to be."

We may never know if the *Fitzgerald* hit bottom on the shoal, but many people believe she did, and that damage from the shoal was the reason she sank. We do know that only about ten minutes later Captain McSorley calls the *Anderson* to report that his ship is now **listing**. A part of the fence on deck is down, and two vents which keep water out of the ballast tanks have been torn off. He tells the *Arthur M. Anderson* that he will slow down to close the gap between the two ships.

An hour has passed and the *Fitzgerald*, leaking and listing, continues on for Whitefish Point. The weather continues to worsen. The waves are twenty-five to thirty feet tall, and the wind blows steadily at sixty to seventy miles an hour with gusts of nearly one hundred miles per hour. The waves come from behind, sweep over the deck, and the water pours down the broken vents into the ballast tanks. Captain McSorley has both of his big pumps going, but they don't keep up with the water rushing into the ship's ballast tanks.

Suddenly a big blast of wind tears away the small mast that holds the radar scanners. The *Fitzgerald* now has only a **radio direction finder** to guide her. A **beacon** on Whitefish Point sends a signal that tells the *Fitzgerald* she's heading in the right direction, but the

The beacon and light on the Whitefish Bay lighthouse failed during the big storm.

signal does not show how far away the ship is from the point. At about 4:30 in the afternoon, the beacon and the light on the point lose electric power and stop. The beacon's backup generator also fails. The *Fitzgerald* is blind!

Captain McSorley calls any ship in Whitefish Bay and ends up talking to a friend who's piloting a Swedish freighter. Captain McSorley's friend asks if the *Fitzgerald* is receiving the signal from the point and can see the light. He doesn't recognize Captain McSorley's voice. Captain McSorley, probably quite shaken by this time, tells his friend, "We are taking heavy seas over our deck; it's the worst sea I've ever been in. We have a bad list and no radar."

The *Anderson* must now act as the *Fitzgerald's* eyes. The two ships stay in radio contact so the *Anderson* can direct the *Fitzgerald*. They are coming near Whitefish Point. Once they pass the point, they will be sheltered from the tremendous waves.

At seven o'clock at night, only seventeen miles and about an hour and a half from shelter, the Anderson calls to tell the *Fitzgerald* that a ship is coming out of Whitefish Bay and will pass them safely to the west. The first mate on the *Anderson* asks Captain McSorley how they are doing with their problems. "We are holding our own," the Captain answers.

It is dark and snowing hard. The *Anderson's* radar shows only a white blob. When the snow stops, Captain Cooper and his mate can see lights from a freighter coming out of the bay, but the *Fitzgerald* is gone!

Captain Cooper calls the U.S. Coast Guard several times, but no one seems worried. After all, 700-foot ships don't just disappear. After trying again and again to contact the *Fitzgerald*, Captain Cooper again calls the Coast Guard and tells them he is very concerned. He says, "I just hope he didn't take a nose dive."

For the *Edmund Fitzgerald* and her crew, the fight is over. She did take a "nose dive," and now lies 530 feet below on the cold, dark, quiet bottom of Lake Superior.

Chapter Six

The Search

All attempts to contact the *Fitzgerald* by radio failed. Finally the Coast Guard accepted the unbelievable, and ordered a search. Unfortunately, the Coast Guard didn't have a ship in the area which was large enough to brave the storm. They asked the *Arthur M. Anderson* and any other ships from as far away as Duluth to respond.

Although reluctant to go back out into the raging storm, Captain Cooper turned his ship around and went to search. The *William Clay Ford* and the *Hilda Marjanne* also went out, but the *Hilda Marjanne* was forced to turn around. Several other ships already on Lake Superior were unable to turn around and search because they were afraid that turning in the heavy seas would cause them to **broach** and roll over.

The search continued for several days. No survivors, not even one body was found. An oil slick on the water marked the approximate place where the *Fitzgerald* was last seen. Empty life jackets, life rings, oars, propane tanks, and bits of lumber were scattered throughout the area. Both fifty-man lifeboats were found empty and ripped apart. They had been torn from the deck as the great freighter went under. The two large life rafts were also found. They were empty.

A wreck that later proved to be the *Fitzgerald* was found by using **side-scan sonar**, a machine that draws pictures of the bottom of the lake. Since divers cannot safely work at 530 feet below the water surface, the Coast Guard decided to send down an unmanned submarine to investigate. The following spring a U.S. Navy **CURV** (Controlled Underwater Recovery Vehicle) went to the bottom of the lake. A CURV is like a sled with electric

The Coast Guard found the wreckage of the ship.

motors to move it around. It has a mechanical arm, and it is attached to a ship above by a cable. This CURV carried video cameras and still cameras to take pictures of the *Fitzgerald.*

A life jacket floats inside the wheelhouse which was bent out of shape when the Fitzgerald sank.

The haunting images that came back showed the front part of the ship sitting upright in mud. A large area of twisted and torn metal that once was the middle of the ship was behind. At an angle and upside down was the back section of the ship. Taconite was spread everywhere.

No bodies could be seen. Through the windows of the pilot house, a lifejacket could be seen floating on the ceiling and the microphone from one of the radios dangled out of the shattered glass. The *Fitzgerald* had gone under so fast that no one was able to radio a distress message.

Chapter Seven

Why Did She Sink?

Why did the *Edmund Fitzgerald* sink? To this day, no one is certain of the reason. The Coast Guard investigation took almost two years. Their investigators viewed the videotape and photos of the wreck. They also interviewed **maritime** experts, the crew of the *Anderson*, former crew members of the *Fitzgerald,* and many others. In the end, the investigators admitted they didn't know why the *Fitzgerald* went down.

The opinion of the Coast Guard investigators was that leaking hatches on the *Fitzgerald* caused the ship to take on water. They believed water from the large waves sweeping the deck entered the cargo hold through bad seals around the hatches. They also believed that some of the hatch clamps may not have been fastened securely.

The investigators guessed that the fence was knocked down and the vents were broken off by something large, perhaps a log, washing onto the deck in the storm. The missing vents allowed more water into the ship. Finally, there was too much water in the ship, and she could no longer stay afloat.

A separate investigation by the Lake Carriers Association, a group of ship owners and operators, reached a different conclusion. This group thought the *Fitzgerald* struck bottom on the Six Fathom Shoals, damaging the ship's **hull**. They believed that Captain McSorley accidentally drove his ship over the shallow area. They argued that if the ship hit bottom, the pressure could have blown the vents up off the deck. As the ship hit bottom the front and back could have sagged, causing the fence wire to snap.

The investigators from the Lake Carriers Association did not think the leaking hatches could have caused the sinking. They believed that if water had simply leaked through the hatches, the pumps would have been able to expel the water. It seemed to them that there must have been a larger leak to cause the ship to fill with water.

Both investigations agreed that the *Fitzgerald*, unknown to her captain and crew, was filling with water for some time before she went under. In the end, with the ship sitting too low in the water, a huge wave, or perhaps several waves rolled forward along her deck and crashed into the forecabin, pushing it down. Possibly, under the weight, one or more hatches collapsed, allowing water to rush in. The last view from the pilot house would have been a wall of water as the ship plunged nose first for the bottom.

The *Fitzgerald* may have gone down in as little as ten seconds. Once she tipped forward, all the water and taconite crashed forward, driving her down. The bow hit the bottom of the lake with tremendous force. The middle of the ship burst apart, spilling taconite over the fore section. The stern of the ship rolled over and came to rest upside down.

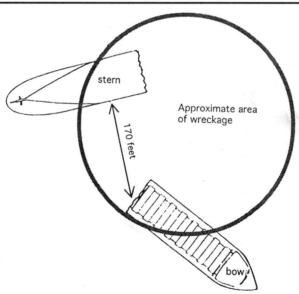

The Edmund Fitzgerald lies in two pieces at the bottom of Lake Superior. The ship's stern is upside down.

This metal plate, where the stern broke away from the midsection, was torn from the rivets.

All hands on the *Fitzgerald* were lost. Any crewmen who survived the violence of the ship going down, could not have survived long on the bottom. The pressure under 530 feet of water would have caused the cabins to flood quickly, drowning anyone who had not already been killed.

"Lake Superior never gives up her dead," is an old saying of Great Lakes sailors. The cold water acts like a freezer and preserves bodies. Micro-organisms that normally cause bodies to decay and float up, cannot work in such cold water. Thus, no bodies of crew members were recovered.

The seamen interviewed by the Coast Guard said that even if the captain and crew had known their ship was sinking, there would not have been much chance to save themselves. All agreed that launching the lifeboats in twenty-five to thirty-foot seas would have been dangerous, if not impossible. In the cold Superior water with only life jackets on, they would have frozen to death in less than a half hour — not enough time to be picked up by even the *Anderson* nine miles behind.

The seamen said the best way to escape would have been to inflate the life rafts, climb inside, and wait for the ship to sink out from underneath them. This is how the survivors of the *Morrell* and the *Bradley* had escaped. But even then, unless they were picked up soon, the men would have died from exposure. Captain McSorley knew his ship was in danger, but he must have felt that the crew's best chance was to steam ahead and try to reach the shelter of Whitefish Bay.

In hopes of preventing another disaster like the sinking of the *Fitzgerald,* some changes have been made in the shipping industry. New ships have monitors built into the hull to detect leaks and stress on the framework. Crew members are provided with survival suits. These thick padded suits are designed to keep them warm and afloat.

Ships now use Loran C, an electronic navigation system that receives signals from stations around the Lakes to give captains an exact location of their ship. An even better system, Global Positioning Systems or GPS, is beginning to replace Loran C. GPS receives its signals from satellites in outer space. Today depth sounders are also much more common on freighters than they were when the *Fitzgerald* sank. This device could have alerted Captain McSorley to the water depth and possible danger at the Six Fathom Shoals.

A year after the *Edmund Fitzgerald* sank, Gordon Lightfoot wrote a song called "The Wreck of the *Edmund Fitzgerald.*" It became very popular and soon was playing on radios all over the country. This ballad tells the story of the final voyage of the great freighter.

Every year, on November 10, a deacon in the Mariner's Cathedral in Detroit reads the name of every crew member lost on the *Edmund Fitzgerald,* while an old ship's bell in the belfry tolls twenty-nine times. It is a way of keeping alive the memory of the crew of the *Edmund Fitzgerald.*

Epilogue

A number of expeditions have sent manned submarines down to visit the wreck since the 1975-76 investigation into the sinking of the *Fitzgerald*. In September 1980, two crewmen from the *Calypso*, Jaques Cousteau's research ship, descended to the cold and dark floor of Lake Superior. At first when they spotted the ship, they were terrified. Light was coming from the cabin window. They quickly realized that the light was only a reflection from their submarine lights. For a half hour they explored the wreckage, then returned to the *Calypso* to continue their research on the Great Lakes.

The summer of 1994 brought more explorations of the nearly twenty-year-old wreck. In June, producer Joe MacInnis sent a manned submersible down to shoot videos and photos for a Great Lakes television program he was producing. Later that same summer, a *Fitzgerald* researcher, Fred Shannon, explored the wreck in a two-man submarine. He gathered material for a videotape and book he planned to produce for the twentieth anniversary of the sinking.

Shannon found what the other explorers were hoping and dreading to find. Partially buried beneath wreckage by the bow, he spotted one of the crewmen. The body, still wearing work clothes, was in fairly good condition. Shannon also saw that the body was wearing a life jacket, evidence that the crew of the *Fitzgerald* knew their ship was in terrible trouble before it plunged to the bottom. Because the life jacket was made of cork, it had proved useless. Below 200 feet, the water pressure squeezes the air out of cork.

Shannon believes the *Fitzgerald* broke up on the surface and may have stayed afloat for as long as five minutes. This theory seems unlikely. If the ship broke in two, as he believes, it seems probable that one or more crewmen would have jumped overboard or into one of the rafts. But no survivors or bodies were found on the water's surface.

The *Edmund Fitzgerald* lies in Canadian waters and is now protected as an underwater historic site. A buoy on Lake Superior's surface marks the spot the wreckage lies beneath the dark cold water.

Remembering the *Edmund Fitzgerald*

During the summer of 1995 an expedition was launched to recover the *Fitzgerald's* bell. The bell was to be placed in a memorial to the ship's crew at Whitefish Point. With the support of the crew's surviving families, two Canadian Navy submersibles, and a diver in a specially designed hardshelled diving suit, the expedition was a success. A replica of the ship's bell with the twenty-nine names of the crew members was left behind on the *Fitzgerald.* The original was restored to the condition of a working bell and dedicated on November 10, 1995, twenty years after the sinking, in a ceremony attended by many of the family members. Efforts are now being made to protect the *Fitzgerald* as an underwater grave to prevent future diving and disruption of the ship and her crew.

Glossary

aft - behind, or the back.

aground - when a ship gets stuck on the bottom of a body of water.

aloft - high up on the masts or in the rigging of a ship.

ballast - weight added to lower a ship in the water, making it less top-heavy.

basin - a depression in the Earth's surface.

beacon - a navigational signal; either a light or a radio signal.

berth - a bed on a ship; also, a job on a ship.

bosun - crew member in charge of the deckhands.

bow - the front of a ship.

breakers - waves breaking on or near shore that are caused by large swells of water tipping over as they approach the shore.

broach - when a vessel rolls onto its side.

cadet - a student in training for a particular crew position.

captain - the commander or head of a vessel.

cargo - the material or goods a ship is carrying.

charts - maps showing safe and unsafe areas of the water; maps detailing water depth, navigational aids (beacons, buoys, etc.), and harbor entrances.

chief engineer - crew member in charge of the ship's engine.

CURV - Controlled Underwater Recovery Vehicle; a sled-like vehicle containing a mechanical arm and cameras.

deckhands - crew members responsible for maintaining the outside of a ship.

depth sounders - devices that bounce sound waves off the bottom of the lake to determine the water's depth under the vessel.

down-bound - ships headed from Lake Superior to the lower lakes; opposite of up-bound.

first mate - the officer next in line of command after the captain of a ship.

foc'sle - the forward cabin on a ship.

fore - forward or at the front.

gale - wind and wave conditions not quite as bad as in a storm.

GPS - Global Positioning System; a very accurate electronic device that receives signals from several satellites and computes an exact location anywhere on Earth.

hands - the crew of a ship.

hold - the area in the bottom of a ship where cargo is stored.

hull - the bottom or a boat or ship.

knot - a measurement of speed; one nautical mile per hour.

leadline - a piece of lead which is lowered into water to determine its depth.

listing - tipping to the side.

locks - compartments in a narrow waterway which can be flooded or drained to raise or lower a ship passing between two lakes of different altitudes.

Loran C - an older electronic device that helps determine position from signals sent out by land base beacons.

mariners - sailors.

maritime - anyting relating to shipping or sailors.

oilers - crew members who care for the engine.

porters - crew members who serve meals and clean the cabins.

radar - an electronic device that sends out radio signals and displays land, other ships, or anything capable of bouncing radio signals back; a device used to determine position and the location of dangerous objects.

RDF - Radio Direction Finder; an electronic device that zooms in on beacons emitting certain radio frequencies and tells the direction of the beacon from the ship.

shoal - a shallow part of a lake or body of water.

side-scan sonar - a machine that draws pictures of the lake bottom.

soundings - measurements of the depth of water.

stern - the back of the ship.

taconite - iron ore found in the Lake Superior region, refined, and formed into pellets.

voyageur - Frenchmen who transported furs by canoe in the Great Lakes region.

watch - crew members who watch for other boats and obstacles.

ways - a track on which ships are built; a track used to launch or slide a ship into the water.

Welland Canal - a waterway constructed to allow ships to travel around Niagara Falls between Lakes Erie and Ontario.

wheelsmen - crew members who steer a ship.

wipers - crew members who clean the engine room.

Museums to Visit

Several maritime museums have photos and artifacts from the *Edmund Fitzgerald*:

Great Lakes Shipwreck Historical Museum
111 Ashmun, Sault Ste. Marie, MI 49783
(906) 635-1742
Located at the tip of Whitefish Point, the museum has artifacts from the *Fitzgerald*, as well as from other ships lost in these treacherous waters. Its director, Tom Farnquist, has played an important role in preserving the ship's history.

Museum Ship *Valley Camp*
Le Sault de Ste. Marie Historical Sites Inc., 501, E. Water St., Sault Ste. Marie, MI 49783
(906) 632-3658
Located in Sault Ste. Marie not far from the Soo Locks, the *Valley Camp* is a retired Great Lakes freighter. Visitors can tour the entire ship and see where the crew once lived and worked. In addition, the enormous cargo hold contains exhibits on the Great Lakes, shipping, and shipwrecks. The remains of the *Fitzgerald's* lifeboats are on display.

Dossin Great Lakes Museum
100 Strand Drive, Detroit MI 48207
(313) 267-6440
Located on Belle Isle in Detroit, this museum has information on the *Fitzgerald* and has one of the anchors lost before her sinking and later recovered from the Detroit River. The pilot house from the SS *William Clay Ford* was recently attached to the Museum and overlooks the Detroit River.

Another museum has information on the history of Great Lakes shipping:

Michigan Maritime Museum
Dyckman Avenue at Bridge, South Haven, MI (616) 637-8078